Copyright © 2021 by Amy Beth Wright and Derek Wright
ISBN 978-1-64662-513-0 First Edition
All rights reserved under International and Pan-American Copyright Conventions. No part of this book may be reproduced in any manner whatsoever without written permission from the publisher, except in the case of brief quotations embodied in critical articles and reviews.

Publisher: Leah Huete de Maines

FLP Editor: Christen Kincaid

Cover Art: Yellowstone National Park, Wyoming. Photo by Derek Wright

Cover and Interior Design: Nicholas Wright

Order online: www.finishinglinepress.com
also available on amazon.com

Author inquiries and mail orders:
Finishing Line Press
P. O. Box 1626
Georgetown, Kentucky 40324
U. S. A.

Wayfinding

Poetry celebrating America's parks and public lands

Edited by Amy Beth Wright and Derek Wright
A collection of poetry from Parks & Points online poetry series

Finishing Line Press
Georgetown, Kentucky

Table of Contents

Contributors 1
Editors' Note 3
Prologue: Trailhead 5
    Yosemite 7
I. Woods and Wilderness 9
Part I. Along the Footpath: Woods and Wilderness 10
The Origin of the National Park Service 13
    Geyser 14
    On This Uncertain Earth 16
    Untamed 17
  No Park Too Small 18
    Breaking Trail At Roxborough State Park, Colorado 19
    Night Hike, Cuyahoga Valley National Park, Northeastern Ohio .. 20
    The Blue Ghost Fireflies of Western North Carolina 21
    Blue Ridge, November 23
    Spire Rock 24
    At Yosemite with Max, Age 6 25
    Hiking to Red Pass 26
  Pitching Camp 27
    Water In The Coals 28
    Camping 29
    First Campout 30
    FIELD GUIDE TO SYCAMORE ISLAND, BLAWNOX, PA 32
II. Water: Wetlands, Marshes, Lakes, and Oceans 35
Part II. Water: Wetlands, Marshes, Lakes, and Oceans 36
    What the Fish Know 37
    Zebra Mussels at Lake Charlevoix 38
    dreaming the land 39
    Road Trip: Indiana Dunes National Lakeshore 41
    Ten Days on the Water 42
    Marblehead 44
    Destruction Bay, Yukon 45
    Rafting the Truckee 46
    Salt Marsh 48
    Sunken Forest, Sailor's Haven 49
  Coastal Waters 50
    Eastern Neck 51
    Lost and Found 52

Seawall	53
Lifespan	54
Wellfeet	55
Marconi Beach	55
Point Judith, Rhode Island	56
Año Nuevo State Park	57
Nisqually Wildlife Refuge	58
Early Autumn at Owen Beach	60
The Changing Light	61
Sunset For Now at Naples, Florida	63

III. Snow, Ice, and Mountains 65

Part III. Extremities: Snow, Ice, and Mountains	66
Throwing Ice at Bolton Landing	67
Winter Lake Erie, New York	68
Below Freezing	69
Sawtooth Mts.	70
Looking Up	71
Fieldnotes in February at Dawn	72

IV. Deserts and Canyons 75

Part IV. Heat and Rock: Deserts and Canyons	76
The Grand Canyon	77
Me in My Jet Fighter	78
Number 395 (Ghost Ranch, Abiqui, New Mexico)	79
Last Gaze on Desert Outlook, Grand Canyon	80
Metamorphism	81
Balsamroot in the Columbia Basin	83
A Stillness Rose	84
Being at Indian Canyon, Agua Caliente, CA	85
Big Bend and the Rio Grande	86
Photograph of You Straddling Two Countries	87
For the Escape and the Bonding	88
Reflecting Pools	90
Written in Stone	92

Epilogue 95

Asset Protection	96
The Trail Back	97
The Poets	**98**
Acknowledgements	**109**
About the Editors	**111**

Contributors

Pamela Ahlen
Mary Ardery
Phillip Bannowsky
Karen Berry
Gary Bloom
Jack C. Buck
Jeff Burt
Pamela Hobart Carter
Amanda Lin Costa
Carol Deering
Ann DeVilbiss
Iris Jamahl Dunkle
Susan Melinda Dunlap
Sara Eddy
Celeste Emmons
Andy Fogle
Laura Foley
Christine Gelineau
Mike Good
Atreyee Gupta
Lois Marie Harrod
Katherine Hester
Emily Alta Hockaday
Alicia Hokanson
Mary Christine Kane

Susan Marsh
Robert McHugh
Kathleen Meadows
Kevin Oberlin
Rebecca Hart Olander
Francis Opila
Carl "Papa" Palmer
Elizabeth Paul
Kristin Bryant Rajan
Cinthia Ritchie
Nicole Robinson
Marian Kaplun Shapiro
Sarah Stern
Virginia Chase Sutton
Dorothy Swoope
Debbie Theiss
Marjorie Thomsen
Kerry Trautman
Gene Twaronite
Kory Wells
Pat Phillips West
Allyson Whipple
Martin Willits Jr.
Sally Zakariya
Tom Zimmerman

Pea Island National Wildlife Refuge, North Carolina. Photo by Derek Wright.

Editors' Note

Our annual online poetry series at Parks & Points revealed two things to us about parks and public lands, be they local, state, or national: because they are shared, they implicitly integrate us within a community beyond oneself, while drawing us back inward, to sharper, clearer insight, understanding, and perspective. Noticing what is within urges us forward in the same way that trail markers and guides do. We hope you will read this book of poetry as if you covering ground on a trail, moving forward through topographies, climates, scents, flora, and fauna; self-awakening, reflection, and transformation bubble under the surface, like the burbling mudpots in the Yellowstone caldera.

Parks of all size, location, and administration within the United States are juxtaposed within the collection, as tiny as a local pier at sunset in Naples, Florida and as sublime as the sprawling Yosemite Valley, flanked with granite monoliths and waterfalls. This trail traverses through city, state, and national parks, scenic waterfronts, lakeshores, and wetlands and piers and spur trails and dramatic overlooks and silent desert and broken, clouded sky and the smell of bacon fat sizzling in a pan and a wily current on the Truckee River in California and the song "you sing on the edge of your love, as you thaw, opening to balsamroot in bloom," as Francis Opila writes, and the "heat and strangeness" of Big Bend National Park, as Liz Paul writes, where the Rio Grande, is, "just a narrow current there, so shallow the boats scraped against the stones." These are but a few of the shared, public places that we will visit in *Wayfinding*.

Prologue: Trailhead

John Brown Farm State Historic Site, New York. Photo by Derek Wright.

Yosemite

By Sara Eddy

I left behind a sad story:
friendships ruined,
love affairs sundered,
a stupid job, and
a new friend made
but left behind on
the last day in Seattle.
I took the bus south,
the Green Tortoise Bus,
with seats removed and
one big mattress where
latter-day hippies played guitar–
I took it south
to Joni's California.
And there, from San Francisco,
I went east to Yosemite
and I felt ancient and undone
until I crawled into the belly
of a fallen sequoia,
felt the soft quiet
earthly dust beneath
my hands and knees, and
began the rest of my life.

I.
Woods and Wilderness

Part I. Along the Footpath: Woods and Wilderness

Wilderness is not always forested—wilderness is any land that sustains itself with minimal human intrusion. On a forested path, trees are but one element; the vital interconnectedness of animals, plants, and microorganisms draws us to trails of all sorts, and reveals surprises and life. At Denali National Park rangers rely on sled dogs to travel through and help maintain the park. The trail to Grinnell Glacier is an almost eight-mile round trip journey from the trailhead, through alpine highlands to one of the last remaining accessible glaciers at Glacier National Park—along the way, while constantly keeping an eye out for grizzly bears, one travels steep mountain ledges and spies Upper Grinnell Lake, an enchanting shade of emerald. Bright Angel Trail descends more than 4,000 feet into the Grand Canyon, with multiple switchbacks to Phantom Ranch, one of the treasured, albeit more treacherous, trails at Grand Canyon National Park. The ascent to Inspiration Point, a birdseye view over Jenny Lake in Grand Teton National Park, is a 7.5 mile hike at more than 6,500 feet of elevation. Regardless of terrain, the body begins to follow the trail's contours instinctively; rugged ascents and heat and distance become unremarkable, momentary digressions from a much longer journey.

Taughannock State Park, New York. Photo by Derek Wright.

Yellowstone National Park, Wyoming. Photo by Derek Wright.

The Origin of the National Park Service

President Ulysses Grant signed the Yellowstone National Park Protection Act on March 1, 1872, preserving more than one million acres of land "from injury or spoliation." The signature set a new and important precedent. Before 1872, the federal government typically transferred appropriated western land to private ownership. However, the 1871 Hayden expedition, directed by government geologist Ferdinand Hayden and accompanied by photographer William Jackson and landscape painter Thomas Moran, prompted Congress toward new measures of land protection. Both artists captured Yellowstone's volcanic landscape and pristine, immense wilderness, mythologizing the region's beauty. The Yellowstone Act also, like most of Westward expansion, further displaced groups from the Shoshone, Blackfeet, Crow, Umatilla, Bannock, Cayuse, Coeur d'Alene, Nez, and Perce tribes, who had survived within the region for centuries. Yosemite, Sequoia, Kings Canyon (originally General Grant National Park) and Mount Rainier National Parks were all designated by 1900, and shortly after the turn of the century, Wind Cave, Mesa Verde, and Glacier National Parks were added to the roster. In 1916, federal stewardship of a growing body of national parks was sorely needed, Woodrow Wilson signed the National Park Service into existence with the National Park Service Organic Act on August 25, 1916.

Yellowstone contains half of earth's active geysers, due to a hot spot in the earth's crust and two recurrent magma domes. It is a vast and scenic wilderness of lodgepole pine forests, alpine meadows, and grassland for some of the largest remaining wild herds of elk and bison in the country, along with the iconic wolves. The 21st century rewilding of Yellowstone has returned the park to its true self, turning from the car-centric tourism of the early 20th century. Still a touchstone vacation destination, the park now shelters an extensive variety of flora and fauna, becoming a place to see geysers and other hydrothermal features as well as extensive wildlife.

Geyser

By Tom Zimmerman

We drank four fingers' width of Idaho
potato vodka, wolfed a hamburger,
slugged beer below the Tetons. Horses begged
like dogs for French fries, mom and daughter, brown
as burning earth and melting with the flow
of images, kaleidoscopic blur
before/behind our eyes. Half-drunk, we legged
it up a switchback on a cliff-face, down
a canyon. Rainbow falls, wildflowers, pines:
each axis vertical, so we could glide
to paradise or slide to hell, the roof
of which we walked in Yellowstone, with lines
of pilgrims, faithfully, to see a fried
white angel flee the earth, redemption's proof.

Yellowstone National Park, Wyoming. Photo by Derek Wright.

On This Uncertain Earth

By Kory Wells

We walk expectantly among the geysers,
the land here like nothing we've known before.
We might as well be on the moon or Mars,
there's so much we can't name,
vague cues we don't recognize
until the moment they spew
like hot secrets. Look how the minerals rise
and shimmer. How the mud simmers
in pastel swaths. How twilight lasts and lasts.

Now, in our room at the open window,
we lie and watch, just watch,
the cool thin air from which like magic
bats appear, scores of them,
to spin and spiral in the pine tops
because we all need to eat, and
isn't a little dancing good for the soul?

In this wilderness we've come to understand
perilous, and more than that, precarious,
and more than that, possible,
which is why we see now,
through the fogged gloaming,
beyond the bats and thick pines,
massive buffalo grazing, and beyond them
a lone chipmunk skittering to its burrow.

Soon it will be dark enough to see
the Milky Way, and a million stars winking
down on this yellow, bubbling earth,
down on our warm forms almost lost
among the soft spots biding their time, hungry
for something we'd rather not name.

Untamed

By Amanda Lin Costa

Because you're drawn to vistas
I choose the macro
exploring moss
on the north side
droplets of water
on tender leaves.

You seamlessly switch lenses
f-stops and shutter speeds
I prefer to open wide
wander in the shadows
fungi found beneath
felled trees
a bud not
yet broken.

At Artist's Point
we hold hands
unable to resist
the river
snaking
for miles
rushing
falling
surreal
animated
refusing
to be captured.

Harriman State Park, New York. Photo by Derek Wright.

No Park Too Small

The national parks: iconic, grand, historic. These are shared between all of us, and for so many, stories accumulate over generations—summers at Yellowstone and Glacier, fall sunsets at Rocky Mountain National Park, springtime along Skyline Drive at Shenandoah National Park in Virginia. While we can all share in national parks, our state and local parks are simply as important as the national monoliths of public lands. Poets capture awe and discovery, and gratitude for the local spaces that are, ultimately, foundations for community, and where one can make discoveries on his, her, or their own terms. We will, from here, pass through regional parks, forests, wetlands, oceanfronts, and lakeshores, pausing within a few of the nation's iconic and defining national parks along the way.

Breaking Trail At Roxborough State Park, Colorado

By Iris Jamahl Dunkle

There are days when life juts out red and raw as sandstone. Think: glaciers did it. Think: those red teeth aren't trying to stain your heart. Here, the wild reeks of sage and pink blooms. It hums in the voices of crickets and bird song. Unseen snakes spell away in the tall grass. But, still you walk forward toward whatever vista you came to see. The meadow where pioneer cabins and their stories fall in on themselves. Try to not get buried. Even deer run, longing for home.

Night Hike, Cuyahoga Valley National Park, Northeastern Ohio

By Kristin Bryant Rajan

Three hours after sunset
we take the Buttermilk Falls trail.
The breeze is gentle
for Ohio in October.
The air heavy with sweet nostalgia
of how quickly seasons cool.
Descending deep into the woods
we marvel at the pantomime around us
how shadows and trees
hold more life at night.

We approach a mound of darkness—
you see a void—the anti-bonfire.
I see a heap of buffalo,
a sacrifice of sorts.
We both see a massive arrow piercing through the textured shade.
We find meaning in the dark shapes of the forest.
As we step closer, our focus sharpens—
a tree has fallen
pulling up the earth and roots with its descent.
We peer beneath ripped earth
the majestic tree on the ground.
Dark, cool, moist
the delicate sinewy strands of roots are white
like stars against the black sky of earth.
We sit beneath in silence.
This tree is protective
even when uprooted.

Cuyahoga Valley National Park, fifty square miles between Cleveland and Akron, is a network of forests, rural farmland, ancient cliffs, ledges, and waterfalls. The Towpath Trail along the historic Ohio and Erie Canal was constructed between 1825 and 1832. The Cuyahoga Valley Scenic Railroad offers a scenic two and a half hour train ride through the park.

The Blue Ghost Fireflies of Western North Carolina

By Mary Ardery

The blue flickers
in the mountain meadow
caught us by surprise.

Their dance held majesty
as much as play, like fairies:
intentional with their mischief.

Oh tactile pulse!
          (theirs)

Oh thrum of light!
          (ours)

Growing up
we called them
lightning bugs.

Their glow was slow
and yellow and easily
trapped. In Indiana,

there were things
I didn't even know
to desire: the way

a man's stubble
burns lips differently
at sea level than 5,000 feet up;

the way some light,
when captured,
lasts only the night

—but other light
burns brighter.
Other light will haunt.

Blue Ridge Parkway, Virginia. Photo by Derek Wright.

The Appalachian Mountains extend more than 600 miles between Pennsylvania and Georgia. They feature the tallest peaks east of the Mississippi River, six national forests, more than 700 species of trees, Shenandoah and Great Smoky Mountains National Park, and an iconic "blue" horizon, due to the release of isoprene, an unsaturated hydrocarbon, from the trees.

Blue Ridge, November

By Sally Zakariya

Up at the cabin we would watch
the seasons change on these old hills.
Summers we'd swim naked in the dark
river where you dove for the lost ring
you never found.

Once, on the dusty river road, a horse
black as the night he ran in pounded
up so close we felt the sweat swing wildly
off him and breathed in the exhalation
of his startled snort.

Soon, snow will cloak the young pines
on the slope below us, glazing
their needles with ice.

Now, our old bodies nestle restful
shape against shape
   soft swell of your belly
      curve of my hip
like hills worn down by time
and the sheer weightiness
of worldly things.

An almost welcome veil descends
on us these short dark days—but in the end
who knows what light may shine.

Spire Rock

By Karen Berry

It rose behind us like broken grey teeth, a fortress
of upthrust granite, casting our cabin into daylight darkness,
our frosted mornings, waiting for sun, inching, climbing,
taking forever to get there, like the future. I came of age
in its stone shadow, dangling my legs over the edge
of a concrete bridge, the raging glacier-fed churn
of the Gallatin River foaming below, blue and white and beckoning.
I roamed alone, singing along with the river's thrum,
watched the sun play with knives, the razor-flash of rays on water.
The stone castle loomed as I forged pined paths
of my own making, watchful of bears, moose, elk.
The highway was near, where I could stick out my thumb
and lose my life. I was only afraid that life would never begin.
My stone citadel was empty. It held no soldiers.
I stayed on the banks, basking on boulders, skipping stones,
spying on chipmunks, wondering at birds, dreaming of foxes.

Spire Rock, near Gallatin Gateway, Montana. Photo by Karen Berry.

The Yosemite Valley was first protected in 1864, essentially as a California state park. It is a magical landscape of giant sequoias, waterfalls, glacially carved granite monoliths, and vast stretches of meadows and wilderness.

At Yosemite with Max, Age 6

By Iris Jamahl Dunkle

We watch the golden net of leaves fall then rise from the tree —suspended against the steep shadows of granite cliffs like golden notes. When he stops I see his eyes gather awe. He will not walk on, is fixed and hungry to watch leaves circle in crisp valley air.

Yesterday, at the Visitors Center we listened to a recorded child's voice speak a history for the Miwok from a diorama filled with plastic ghosts, then, we sat, in a small redwood kotcha, his body close, his questions circling mine, circling the stories we had heard. In this sweet darkness there was the scent of earth between history and what's been forgotten.

The valley is a granite bowl where the past still burns a cold silver thread through impossible stone, under a one-eyed moon. Those born here fought to the death to stay.

This is what we do not say. Golden words like leaves netted in air. Lost, but continually returning.

Yohhe'meti (Southern Miwok) or Yos.s.e'meti (Central Miwok) originally referred to the Indian tribe that lived in Yosemite Valley. Yosemite means literally "those who kill."

Hiking to Red Pass

By Pamela Hobart Carter

Late summer, almost fall, it's like I've found my childhood
tucked under these cedars—

and I am ten and lazing on hot stone, watching ants.

For the first time in a long time I feel safe,
now I know the old granite wall always

waits for my remembering, somewhere at my physical center,

available, with you on this hike, or even at my city desk
as I scrounge for perfection

(click sites for research, recheck links and spelling

as if these secure a famous future where you hear me,
and everyone gathers to listen to my wisdom).

The past is contained in our dark insides,

coded in chemicals which replace daily. Somehow they flow
the known channels.

The way sentences store a truth even if unwritten.

All day, anywhere, we may dive back to then.
At the pass we gaze north and south.

We see into spaces where time is slow to round mountains.

Alpine Lakes Wilderness, Commonwealth Basin is in the Cascade Mountains region just outside of Seattle, Washington.

Charles M. Russell National Wildlife Refuge, Montana. Photo by Derek Wright.

Pitching Camp

In the wilderness, a turn or two off the park road, with your car parked a few yards from your tent, day slips into night, and the flame of the campfire slowly dwindles. Logs crumble into a nest of gray and white glowing embers. The embers slowly burn out, leaving a bed of ash in the firepit. The stars stretch infinitesimally across the navy night sky. There is something magical about tent camping. Camping offers a feeling of accomplishment in shedding the comforts of home, and stripping life to a few elements: a tent, a campsite, a flame for cooking a meal, a chair for watching day ease into dusk, gathering to sing or talk, or to think and feel, experiences and memories settling into the body and mind unforgettably.

After I got married, my wife and I would drive up from Minneapolis and camp in the Superior National Forest in Northern Minnesota, often at the same campsites where I went when I was a kid. This poem was inspired by a camping trip to the Boundary Waters Canoe Area in Superior National Forest. We continued to go camping there until we moved to New Orleans in 1983.–Gary Bloom

Photo by Gary Bloom.

Water In The Coals

By Gary Bloom

We look to the woods for our privacy and answers.
All thoughts are burned in the evening fire, and
the bacon grease we wash away beneath
the rusted pump, turning to hard
white ivory in the water,
suddenly ignites in the pan,
leaving no decisions to be made.
We eat our bacon in the dark,
quiet except for a few waves
and the fire gasping for
breath between buckets of water
and then we move
silently beneath the thick patched cloth
the musty canvas smell
the wood smoke in our hair
surrounds us without a sound
but a few waves
and water steaming in the coals.

Camping

By Martin Willitts Jr

1.
An ember in a smothered campfire
snap-cracked its last breath.
A movement of stars
hunches over the charcoal clouds.

The world closed in
like a tent.

The sum total of my life, this infinity
beyond stars where frightened lives
and smallness exist, overtook me.
There was no fear that was not my own.

My heart is always restlessly disturbed.

2.
When in the landscape of dreams,
that quiet presence,
respond to the world
and all its fleeting assurances.

We are strangers even to ourselves.
We could burn and turn cold as coal.
We could go into storm-fields
trying to brush away low-hanging branches
like a person fighting sleep. And still,
we could be seething within silence
as snow reminds us firmly
it is time to hibernate.

3.
To the west,
I knew a mountain by touch.

The sky is greying.
A freeze is coming,
arriving late.

First Campout

By Kerry Trautman

The tent's taut nylon flapped, crackled

    in night's variable winds.

In the distance, thunderstorms

    had moved on eastward.

The baby slept fitfully,

    barely relaxing into steady breaths,

dreaming, perhaps, of lightning

    just beyond the soggy meadow

    with its shrieking red-wing blackbirds,

or of the campfire and its

    new-found, threatening beauty,

waking intermittently in the unfamiliar dark

    with its shuddering, movable walls,

groping for my face,

    grabbing hold with both sweaty palms,

pressing his forehead to my cheek,

    searching, in my skin, for a way home.

Nestled outside of Toledo on the banks of Lake Erie, the trails and beach at Maumee State Park in Oregon, Ohio are beautiful in all seasons. The park preserves some of the last vestiges of unspoiled marshland on Lake Erie, the second smallest of the five Great Lakes.

*Head of Sycomore Island, Blawnox Pennsylvania.
Photo by George Schnakenberg, Jr. / CC BY-ND 2.0.*

Parks often dissolve, or share, the boundary between land and water. Sycamore Island Beach, a 14-acre sliver of land nestled in the Allegheny River just east of Pittsburgh, is in the confluence of water and land, of two worlds, forest and river. The tiny island has more than doubled in size 1809. Earlier in the twentieth century, Sycamore Island, a thriving bird sanctuary, and Nine Mile Island, also in Allegheny, was under the stewardship of the Audubon Society of western Pennsylvania.

FIELD GUIDE TO SYCAMORE ISLAND, BLAWNOX, PA

By Mike Good

For Rick Duncan and Allegheny Land Trust

Morels break into damp spring light
      past the three-trunked sycamore
on the channel-side where river traffic

flows, past the great blue heron nest
      rising above the pebbled shore. Coal
barges tear silty loam and leave river

rocks for the Allegheny to hawk
      and swallow, where turkey vultures sun
their wings like black crosses on electric

trees, where cedar waxwings trill
      inside the Indian cigar tree. Scratched
spicebush potpourri. Orange

impatiens exploding. Do not live
      like the wolf spiders in the storage silo
dining on tadpoles, never knowing

the dredge spoils that rise above the jet

        skis and the fishing poles, never drinking

the sumac tea that boils into red paint or

holding the delta of green cottonwood

        leaves that twist and conspire, never

rising with the ailanthus toward

the canopy sprouting neckbeards

                about girdled cambium

as our island

        slowly deposits

                itself down the river.

I could

        open my eyes and peel

                grapevines off softwood.

I could break down

        at any second.

                I could smell acrid water

pouring from the discharge.

        I could see

myself burning in the sky.

        I could have been an eagle.

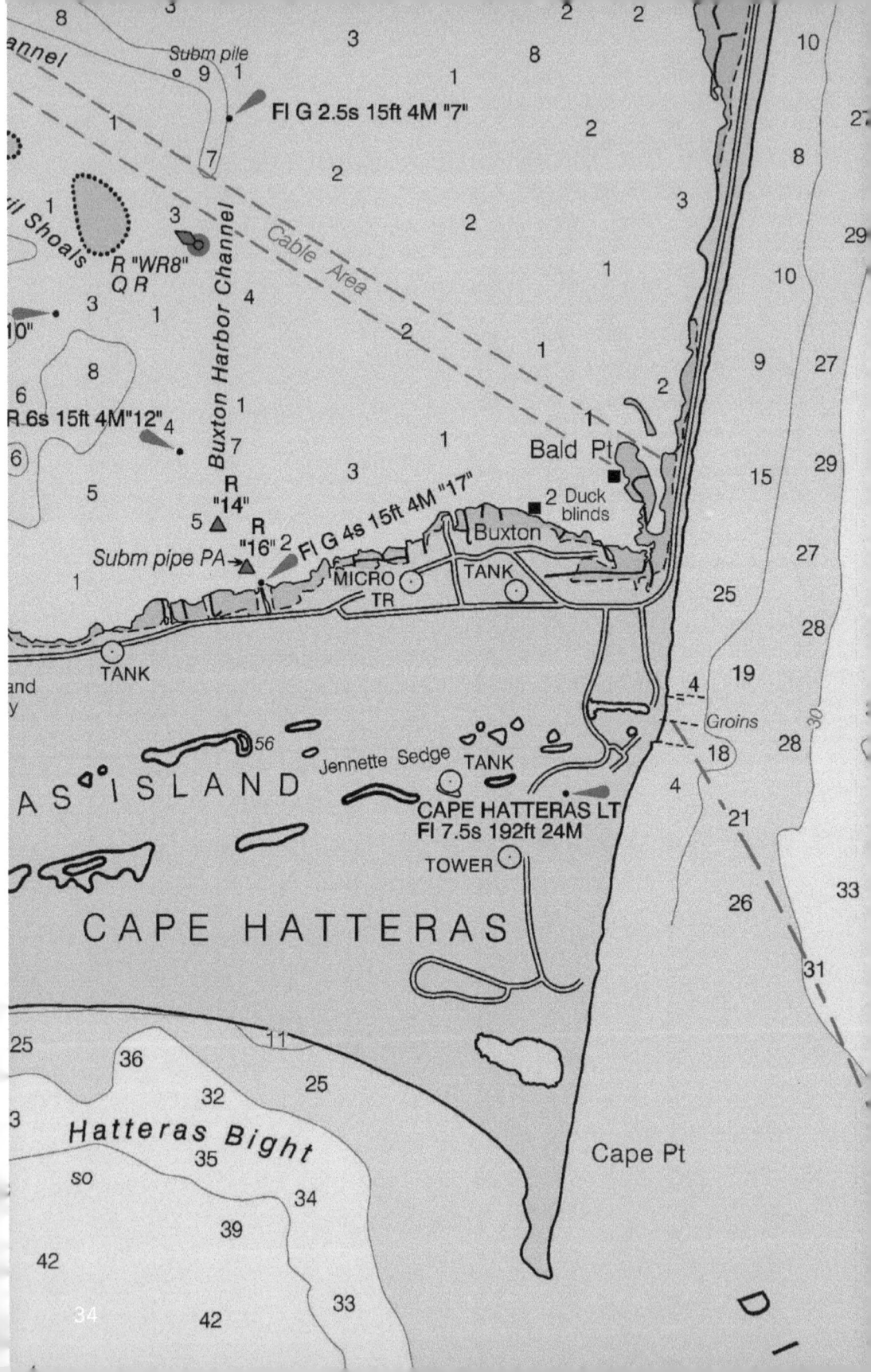

II.
Water: Wetlands, Marshes, Lakes, and Oceans

Part II. Water: Wetlands, Marshes, Lakes, and Oceans

Water is a journey point, a place to grasp at the unending stretch of the ocean or to navigate a trail by following the flow of a river. Water is also critical for sustaining all forms of life, as these poems help us to remember. The bodies of water here are varied, as are their purposes. Many are the connective tissue binding the world of the park to the coastline, as streams, creeks, marshes, ponds, rivers, wetlands, and lakes criss-cross trails and flow to the coasts, "spinning down over deep pools where the river slows" (Alicia Hokanson), "an out-stretched arm reaching toward the depths of Puget Sound" (Pat Phillips West), "until what's left is the flatness of things" (Sarah Stern), and "We fall asleep, our dreams washed in gauzy green, weaving miracles of timeless time where sky becomes ocean, where now becomes forever…" (Marian Kaplun Shapiro).

Virgin Creek Falls Trail, Girdwood, Alaska. Photo by Derek Wright.

What the Fish Know

By Ann DeVilbiss

The morning lake
is a calm blue nothing,
soft horizon, reaching,
early light cutting
through small waves like
a net scrimmed over
        the shallow places.

Our feet move,
pale clumsy giants, and
even the hungriest fish
        skirt away, shy back
to the murky gloom
among the green reeds,
wait for
        better quarry,

as if they remember
how we take them
        inside our cheeks like
        sins or secrets,

as if they remember
        how fish drown in air:

first blood beads up
along the edges of the gills,
the neck flecked pink
with blood's reaching,
then white with the foam
        that gathers along
the heaving sides.

Their scales are
sharp as teeth when
        we weigh them
        in our hands.

Ann DeVilbiss wrote this poem while spending time on the beaches of Lake Michigan, just north of Onekama, Michigan. Here the lake and shore begin their march to the wilds of northern Michigan, the lake deepening as it heads north. The sand dunes are enormous, and in winter, the wind howls, spraying frozen water along the shore.

Zebra Mussels at Lake Charlevoix

By Mary Ardery

I turned inward as Indiana hills and cornfields transformed
into a blur of Michigan cherry orchards and skinny pines.
Nine hours with Mom, Dad, and two older sisters who preferred

music to talking. At the cabin, Cousin Sarah was eager to play.
All day we hauled treasures from the fresh water: bucket
after colorful bucket of zebra mussels. We pried them open

with our small fingers to collect the oozing reward—
the invasive species' inedible meat. Such viscosity was kept
like a secret inside those striped shells known to slice soles

if one day you forgot your water shoes. It was an early study
of exterior vs. interior: a casing that draws blood
but when cracked the right way, yields to something delicate.

Elephant Butte Lake State Park is New Mexico's largest state park, at 43 miles long and 40,000 acres, and contains New Mexico's largest body of water.

dreaming the land

By Susan Melinda Dunlap

a wanderer tramped through the hills
as of days of old
my name is Martin, he said to the chickens he saw
he said it to the lake
the lake turned away
the chickens pecked on and laid their eggs
the wanderer slept on a ledge
but nothing came to his mind's eye
he dove into the lake
into the moon's tail
he stared at stars from beneath the surface
flicked water at moon craters
he pricked his finger on a bottle cap
just some floating flotsam
and whispered
I am another's dream

Covering 15 miles of lakeshore on Lake Michigan, the third largest of the Great Lakes, Indiana Dunes National Park (formerly a national lakeshore) is more than dunes and stunning lake views—trails meander through forests, grasslands, and wetlands.

Road Trip: Indiana Dunes National Lakeshore

By Kristin Bryant Rajan

After a long night,
an empty stomach,
relentless winds,
sleeping on a stick,
hidden from your touch
by thick layers
of sweaters, sleeping bags, hats, and scarves,
I wake to light in Indiana.

Birds and squirrels
rustling through soggy leaves
atone for a tent that will not stand,
a toilet that will not flush.
The cold Midwest wind in early spring
building mountains of sand
can also blow away
the burdens of this journey.

I venture to the woods alone
crawling deep inside the morning darkness of this forest,
climbing hills that grip my thighs
and give me back my breath,
then bumbling down again,
struggling to keep pace with dumb feet
skipping, flying
hoping more than breakfast
to maintain always this momentum.

Running with the rhythm of birds' songs
I find light and breath
with the sunrise.

Ten Days on the Water

By Virginia Chase Sutton

The leader is stuck with me as his canoe companion,
as I lack strength to paddle far. Noah slices
choppy water with an easy stroke. We are first,
a rag-tag group of canoes behind us, unable to keep up.
They are kids I went to high school with but did not know

because I was mostly alone. The biology teacher
and his wife are chaperones. Once in a while,
Noah pulls the canoe over, waits for everyone
to catch up, wants to give us all treats, like seeing
golden wildflowers climbing the edges of a rocky

island or watching a group of floating loons. He pulls ahead
again, a gleaming god in our silver canoe, large pack
between us, me at the head, doing my level best not to
embarrass myself too badly. When we stop, we float, waiting
for the others to appear. He converses, and I answer

his questions about me going to college in a few weeks while
he tells me about Purdue. He enjoys my rapt attention. For lunch,
canoes gather. We eat peanut butter sandwiches and prunes.
Evenings we cook something instant over a fire, with Noah
later climbing the tallest tree to stash our pack of food

away from bears. A tent for females and one for males,
though Noah has his own hidden away. I grow close to him.
I love his easy laugh and silences, his muscled body.
He is a tanned fantasy. One afternoon, when we turn a corner
far from everyone else, he says, come here. I carefully

edge my way to him, shaky on shimmering water. Bend closer,
he says, and stands, pulling me in. It is my first real kiss.
I love tasting his warm tongue, and I tremble back to my post.
The loneliness of being with strangers slips away. I have a secret
now, something every female on this trip would like to have.

The sky pops blueness over clear water. Here, he says,
smiling. He hands me a cup of water dipped from the lake.
Our hands meet and we reach for another kiss. I nearly
drop the silver cup into icy water, not anticipating his
wildly tender gaze as we float nowhere, nearly dinnertime.

Voyageurs National Park is at the upper reaches of Minnesota, where, from the right vantage, one can gaze into Canada. A few developed areas allow for easy recreation; a particularly beautiful journey is through backcountry or backwater, where one can adventure via canoe and not see any other humans for hours, if not days. Even in winter, the ice trails draw hearty adventurers.

Marblehead

By Kerry Trautman

The lighthouse lamp is dark,
and the caretaker's shack—their insides locked,

shuttered from thunder, mayflies,
and the always always

wind. Young, I was willing to teeter on slick seaweedy
boulders, calf-deep

in the cold, Lake Erie side of the waves—
not the calm Sandusky Bay

side of childhood, of railway howls,
of Grandpa's coal-dock towers,

of perch fishing off
Uncle Tom's Lyman. I knew the water dropped off

deep somewhere, hard with earth's cold
minerals. Kelly's Island

on the horizon, with its snakes.
Canada beyond, with caribou and glaciers.

Older now, I would be willing to abandon
my inland

everything, for a post-war bungalow where
families summered away

from the bottle factory, shipyard
and schoolhouse. I would plant a peach orchard,

stitch a kite, allow constant wind and gulls to weave
through my clapboards, gust me

with wet sand and walleye, and wait for
the light to be restored.

Built in 1921, Marblehead Lighthouse is the oldest that is still in continuous operation on the Great Lakes.

Destruction Bay, Yukon

By Cinthia Ritchie

Fog fills the water,
it's hard to see the mountains,
we've been camped here for days,
your body so familiar it feels
like my own skin, ordinary, warm,
the surprise of no surprises,
we swim through nights without
darkness, wake to
eagles down the beach,
bear prints around the tent,
we hang our food from tree
branches,
drink dirty water,
sit on the shore until we lose
our capacity for words,
mouths, meanings,
out here with the wind,
the waves,
the long cool stretches,
and wild.

Rafting the Truckee

By Alicia Hokanson

Set upon blue pontoons
that twitched like dousing rods
we went spinning down
over deep pools where the river slows
marshy fescue and clotted eelgrass along the banks
water clear over silted boulders
and waterlogged pines
went spinning past guys
stomach-flopped on inner tubes
past fishermen knee-deep casting into pools
rods pulling red lures against the green
past ducks scurrying toward us begging
diving for thrown wafers

we slid over brown gravel
where water ran swifter in narrow runnels
into the little thrill of white water
gasps in the rapids
nudging rocks and swirling around them
not quite making the angle we aimed for
hitting all the obstacles
rocks   low bridges   brushy
margins with their hidden sticks
bumping over the scrape
and crunch of the shallows

we wanted the center
but the rudderless tube would not hold it
and toward the end
when the wind came up
our forward strokes did nothing
we spun lazily or furiously
until the river caught us in its line—

even in the last long rapid
pulling hard for the takeout
what carried us
was relentless
clear water moving
all the way down

The Truckee River originates from high within
California's Sierra Nevada range and flows
through Lake Tahoe, into the Truckee River
canyon, and to the Reno metropolitan area.
It crosses miles of Nevada high desert before
flowing into Pyramid Lake, 40 miles northeast of
Reno–there, the water collects, seeps further into
the ground, or evaporates under the Nevada sun.

Salt Marsh

By Emily Hockaday

Sober, I see this island
for what it is. I have always
been able to be still
here. Tonight at dusk
the mosquitos were thin
so we ventured out to the marsh
on the bay side
and watched fish jump
in the small clearings
of marsh grass. Animals come
and go; populations swell
and plummet; dominance
is always passing along. This
is a healthy, moving
ecosystem.

After my father died,
the ecology of my brain
became flooded with adrenaline,
and I am still trying
to rebalance the chemicals.
An animal bone
rests on the side of
the boardwalk—left
by a fox. I haven't seen one
yet, but they are deep
in the dune foliage. Predators
are vital to the health
of this community. The bone
is curved—a lone, open parenthesis.

Fire Island National Seashore occupies 26 miles of Fire Island, a barrier island off of the Long Island coast. White-tailed deer quietly pick their way through grass on high sand dunes at sunset, and the Fire Island lighthouse preserves one of six Fresnel lenses built in 1819. More than 200 plant species and fourteen major vegetation types thrive, from scrubs to thickets to broadleaf forest to wetlands and marshes.

Watch Hill, Fire Island National Seashore. Photo by Derek Wright.

Sunken Forest, Sailor's Haven

By Emily Hockaday

Limbs fall off
leaving knotted eyes
looking out from the forest.
The ecology of this sandy island
was always preparing
for a future
in which it didn't exist. Is that
what I'm doing, too?
I grab the baby's hand
to keep her beside me
while I can. The thick holly canopy
is surprisingly high.

Cape Hatteras National Seashore, North Carolina. Photo by Derek Wright.

Coastal Waters

On the Atlantic and Pacific coasts are scenic and historic oceanfront parks and assorted local, state, and national seashores. To the west, major parks include San Juan Island National Historical Park and Olympic National Park in Washington, the Channel Islands off the coast of Santa Barbara, where kelp forests sustain more than 1,000 species of plants and animals, as well as Redwood National Park, Point Reyes National Seashore and the Golden Gate National Recreation Area in northern California. To the east, the Maine coast, home to Acadia National Park and Saint Croix Island International Historic Site, is one of the world's most dramatic and picturesque rocky coastal shores, ideal for tidepooling, boating, swimming, sunsets, and whale watching. At national seashores like Assateague, Fire Island, and Cape Hatteras, one can linger between land and water, the horizon in the far distance, the deepening ocean in front and the sloping, contoured land behind. Coastal waters express two worlds—the serenity of slackness and stillness, and constant movement.

Eastern Neck National Wildlife Refuge is a 2,285 acre island that is managed as part of the Chesapeake Marshlands National Wildlife Refuge complex.

Eastern Neck

By Kevin Oberlin

Pant legs turned up she wades
out into the Chesapeake,
the marsh quiet around the cold inlet

like a dormant lung encased
in vines and felled trees,
remnants of winter,

the water's pressure on her whitened ankles
less a pull than the soft suck of barnacles
on driftwood and broken rocks.

She submerges an amaretto bottle,
a bulbous fish she fills with sand and shells,
the round stones she has gathered,

a still-life captured in glass,
a costless substitute for a souvenir,
the purple label's edges peeled back

from skin as she draws the bubble up,
water skimming the dark hairs of her arms
toward its free fall from her elbows.

The gift is not in this sip of ocean,
but how sunlight streams from her body
like a wing as she looks toward the shore.

Lost and Found

By Laura Foley

On my sophomore science field trip
to the rocky Maine coast,
I sat captivated by a tidal pool, a little village
of crawling crabs, snails, starfish darting,
a sea anemone appearing to sing.
I stayed so long, I forgot the rising tide,
my teachers, classmates waiting
on the bus. On the exam,
I couldn't calculate the pitch of waves,
or chemical composition of anything,
but I knew how to lose myself
in the world of tiny shifting things.

Acadia National Park, Maine.
Photo by Derek Wright.

Seawall

By Christine Gelineau

My first trip to Mount Desert Island was the summer
I turned twenty, four Augusts after the August
my mother died. A camping trip with the friend
who would one day become my sister-in-law.
Our first day on the island we picked up
a hitchhiker, young guy from Bleecker Street
in the Village, visiting Acadia as we were.
Caution tells us we should never have
opened ourselves to him like that—how impossible
it is now to explain the generational trust we felt then,
what we read in one another's clothes and hair.
The woman I would know for the rest of my life
and the young man we would never see again
roamed the park, contentedly, platonically,
while he took a veteran's pleasure in showing us
where the sweetest blueberries clung
to their granite escarpment, where the mudflats
plump with quahogs were. None of us seemed
to know the skies well enough to have heard
of the Perseids, but he knew Seawall and on our last
night there we carried blankets out to muffle
the stony beach, and lay down in the dark, rocked
by the lapping of the unseen waves, easy together
beneath the shower of frolicking stars.

Acadia National Park on Mount Desert Island in Maine coalesces sandy oceanfront, coastal rocky headlands, bays, inlets, granite ridges, lakes, ponds, forested wilderness and mountains, wetlands, marshes, swamps, and 27 miles of historic motor roads, 158 miles of hiking trails, and 45 miles of carriage roads within 47,000 acres along the Atlantic Ocean.

Lifespan

By Marian Kaplun Shapiro

The curtain rises: Summer. Maine. A screen door.

luna moth   soft-glowing
         pistachio wings trembling   sound-
           less waiting waiting one week
                 (Is today day one?)   and

then what?

So quiet now. The humans have blasted off,
freedom exploding like champagne uncorked, rocketing to
golftennisbikingwaterskiinghikingswimming…
                                           except for

 me. Sitting. Keeping company with
the occasional loon. The lone duck.
                             The

lake.
    Mountain.
       Sky.
Cabin,
     a little ways uphill
One room for sleepingeatingwashingwritingreading. Family. After dinner
parlor games. Cards. Telling when-I was-your-age stories of our wild years
to the kids//grandkids who can't quite take it in. Really? No, really? They
shake their middle aged/ adolescent heads, preparing to facebook their friends
the moment they rejoin their iPhones at their nearby little rental houses.

You and I
wait quietly. Together. We turn, almost as one, to find the luna moth
flickering almost imperceptibly like a Yahrzeit candle in its final hour.
We fall asleep, our dreams washed in gauzy green, weaving miracles
of timeless time where sky becomes ocean, where now becomes
forever….
                                                  ….In the morning
she is gone. For where? The question is a nesting doll in which
each answer will reveal another mystery. It gets louder by the minute.

Wellfeet

By Rebecca Hart Olander

On the upland heath above Marconi,
I watch a hawk keying into prey
over broom crowberry and poverty grass,
above the ocean swelling with seals
and the two souls a great white and
browning storm waves took into the dark.
Controlled fire sustains this terrain—
management by match.
After small burns, a renewal
of native brush, thicket of ground shrub.
Could it be the same with us?
Gutted, glutted, casualties of argument.
After we've destroyed each other,
could cinder conjure a new start?

Marconi Beach

By Sarah Stern

Midnight moon so bright
it made night
the negative of night.

Waves, late August,
foaming, the same mistakes
over and over

until what's left
is the flatness of things:
this black stone worn down,

the beach grasses too,
the horizontal lovers
beyond the break.

Created by glaciers and drift, Cape Cod National Seashore is a forty-mile stretch of shoreline with marshes, ponds, uplands, historic lighthouses, and wild cranberry bogs.

Point Judith is at the origin of Narragansett Bay, where the tidal mixing of open ocean waters with bay waters creates a choppy patch of ocean. Several ships have sunk in the area, and the Point was also the site of a sea battle in which the U.S. sunk a German U-Boat in the final days of World War II. Nearby on Newport Island is the Vanderbilt mansion and The Breakers, designed by Richard Morris Hunt.

Point Judith, Rhode Island

By Marjorie Thomsen

On a overnight field trip with my son and his class,
the counselor says to lay flat with our bellies against
the damp wooden dock, our eyes over the salt pond.
The fifth graders can't tamper with the October
stars or squish the almost-full moon. There's clarity
to the night making the dock floor feel holy—an ancient
cathedral wall laid out beneath our jacketed bodies.

The counselor-scientist speaks firmly but softly
of plankton's wonder, the gravity of keeping
our flashlights off. She pronounces bioluminescence
in the language of love. With strict instruction,
we stroke the surface of the water with the tips
of our fingers. Like a magic trick, the water sparkles
silvery light; boys cry out *fairy dust!* and inches
from our faces are the smallest signs of life.

Año Nuevo State Park

By Jeff Burt

At year's end we hike from a silent old creamery
siding faded to a butter yellow
down to the raucous Pacific coast.
The marine fog layer descends
on an unseen zip line running
north to south, a forbidding darkness
yielding to warm splashes of sunshine.

Using seagulls as markers,
we follow lowland until we must rise
out of grass and scrub sage
to climb dunes, and, there, first,
a young male elephant seal
asleep on sand, then an exhausted second.

When we mount the final dune

O massive snorting flesh!

O the drop-jawed awe!

struck by the colossal herd,
a thousand in congregation
in a single view, weaners motive
while mothers snore, slumber,
lumber for a free spot,
a lone bull sneezes, snickers,
squawks, his stuttering thunder
caroming off cliff walls,
a roar of loneliness, of request,
of ambition, of defeat.

This stretch of California beachfront just north of Santa Cruz is home to one of the largest breeding grounds for elephant seals and draws crowds to view these massive sea mammals fight for dominance, as well as their small pups as they emerge into the world. The park preserves undeveloped shoreline and also features inland trails.

Nisqually Wildlife Refuge

By Pat Phillips West

Cool, crisp air nips at my face, as I start
from the trailhead by the visitors' center
My feet know the way, finding their rhythm
step by step. Sometimes the bones of my life
feel heavy, but in my heart along with sinew,
muscle and blood, there's a receptor
that connects me to this land
and those who came before me.

A short way on the Twin Barnes Loop,
nature's rock star perches in the afternoon sun
at the very top of a pine tree.
I use my binoculars to watch the bald eagle
slowly lift off. He holds his wings almost
completely flat rarely flapping and soars
higher than any other bird. Wonderstruck

I continue, the path winds through wetlands
where ducks paddle around in emerald-green algae
that looks like the surface of another planet.
Further along, a blue heron stands motionless,
so busy with his own happiness.

The wetlands give way to forest, light and shadow
dance across my skin. Here branches overlap
like fingers folded in prayer. I look up at the sun
shining through gold and yellow leaves
a stained-glass window in nature's cathedral.
The moment so wide and so deep.

I come to the wood plank boardwalk
jutting into the marshland a full mile—
an out-stretched arm reaching toward
the depths of Puget Sound. I feel an ease
in my body as I walk the length
to the viewing platform. I take pleasure
in the long trough of silence
to eavesdrop as earth speaks to sky.

Nisqually National Widlife Refuge, Washington. Photo by Pat Phillips West.

Early Autumn at Owen Beach

By Carl "Papa" Palmer

Tacoma Washington rains
a foggy mist I breathe
in cadence
with soft whispers
of Puget Sound surf
heard front row center
sitting on this sand-locked log
all to myself at Owen Beach.

Seeking similes for birds
behaving like birds
as I float a morning prayer
toward the Tahlequah ferry
crossing for Vashon Island
from Point Defiance Park
sailing the horizon between
gray water and gray sky.

An older park in Tacoma, Washington, the beach is part of Point Defiance Park. The Army turned over the property in the late 19th century, starting a century and half of use as one of the most popular parks in the city.

The Changing Light

By Kathleen Meadows

Last night I saw the changing light
pink-luster like the inside of a conch shell
      hauled from the beach, collecting time
      its shell crystals primordial dust—
perhaps the last gasp of a dying galaxy,
small pinpricks of ancient light
flowing like water carving the hillsides
behind Mt. Tam.

I stood and watched the clouds of Marin,
moving methodically over the hills,
      like a medieval scholar scouring the heavens.
I could see across the bay, find my rooftop,
touch the tips of my tallest redwood trees, spot
my cat playing with a fallen baby squirrel.

I saw the light change to deep crimson at the
horizon, soft purple bands melting silhouettes
sharpening my gaze on the fog-blanketed Headlands,
lights from the red bridge haloed across Sausalito
motioning me back to the last waning light above,
the first stars stitched onto blue-black tapestry
like primitive beacons, signaling me home.

Bahia Honda State Park, Florida. Photo by Derek Wright.

Sunset For Now at Naples, Florida

By Andy Fogle

Check, check. All the standard elements
are here: sea-sky horizon, the small-shelled
shore-lip, scattered palms, a happily
zig-zagged pier, a boulder jetty
that works for now. It's like walking through
a photo album: a father holding
his small daughter, then hands with his wife,
who later chase-stalks her son. The whole
family of four, framed by these tokens
and an aging man's squint, who is three things
to these four people—father, father-
in-law, grandfather—and his tremor
does not for now. Pan the scene: a group
of twenty-somethings timing their leap
for the camera on a tripod; a man
with a construction company t-shirt
teaches his son to surf; smokers fume
on the wood steps leading from lot to sand;
retirees in lawn chairs with coolers
of boxed wine and cutting boards. In a few years,
some of these kids will be big, some of these
elders ash, and vice versa. They've gathered
to witness another day pass. The air
is stable and clear, the light less scattered,
so when the sun slips, they glimpse the green flash,
treasured mirage, and then, for now, they all applaud.

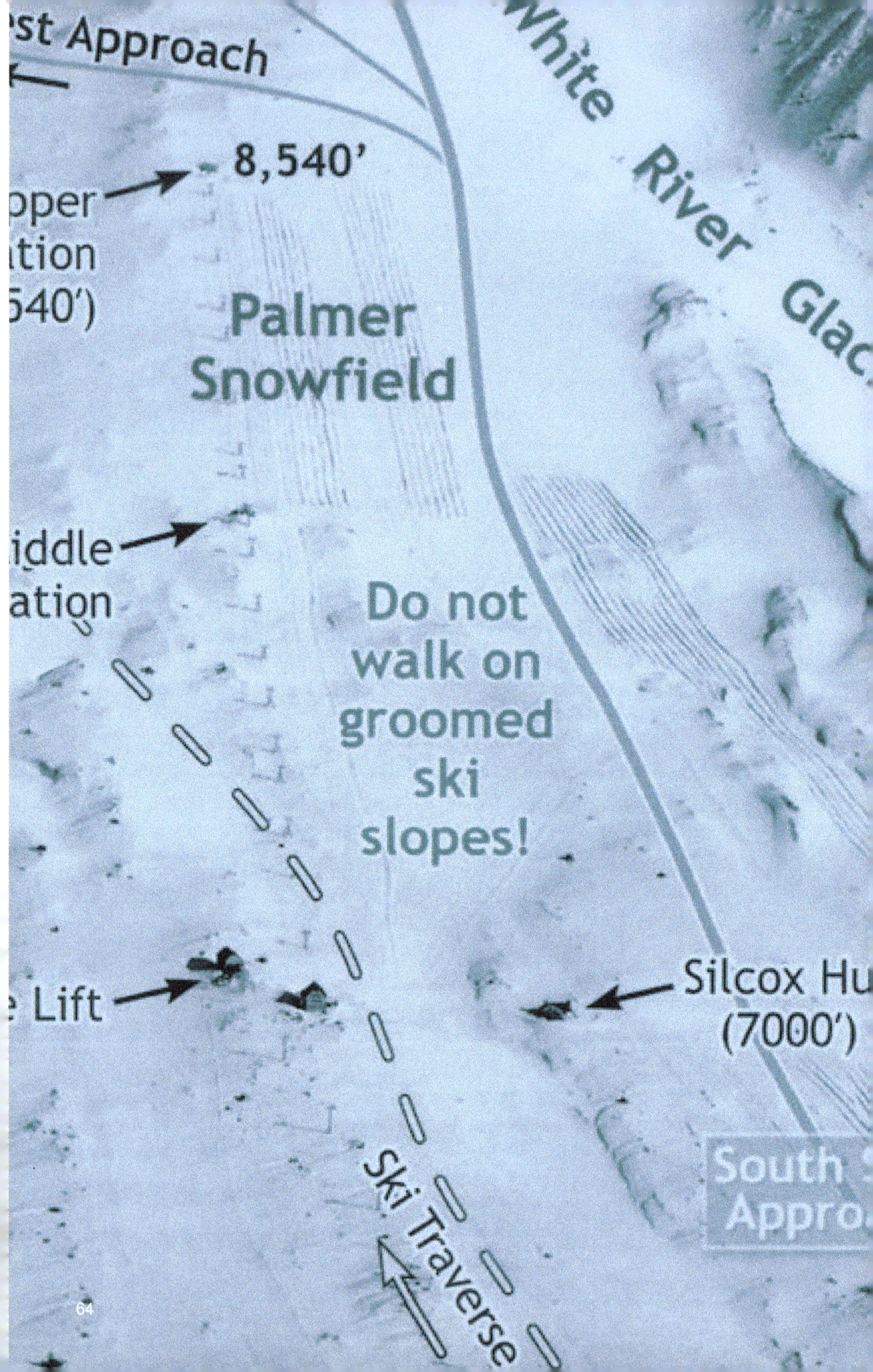

st Approach
White River Glac
8,540'
pper
tion
540')
Palmer Snowfield
iddle
ation
Do not walk on groomed ski slopes!
Lift
Silcox Hu
(7000')
South
Appro
Ski Traverse

III.
Snow, Ice, and Mountains

Part III. Extremities: Snow, Ice, and Mountains

Some of the most iconic and memorable parks have snow, ice, and mountains as their core. From the glacially-carved pointed peaks in the Alaskan and western national parks like Grand Teton, North Cascades, and Glacier to the slowly-rounded-by-millennia peaks at Great Smoky Mountains National Park, the austerity of the mountains places all other things in perspective. They invite a slow climb, a more extreme adventure, or a long, ruminative experience. Today, the march of ice at Glacier Bay National Park can be seen as massive chunks of glaciers calve off into the sea. Snow and ice still bring change to parks and public lands, in a way that allows the landscape to tell another story, of expanse and cool hues, of reflection and fortitude.

Grand Teton National Park, Wyoming. Photo by Derek Wright.

Throwing Ice at Bolton Landing

By Andy Fogle

The lake is thawing in slabs on the shore.
March, and we've come here on a whim to see
what it's like in an opposite season.
No one here, the playground like a widow,
the restrooms locked tight, but water and sky
are one blue, in counterpoint shades.
It's a hard shine on this small flat of muck,
after months of loss after loss, turn
upon turn, when we have not often
"been ourselves," none of us. Like others, this
is slow to change, its temperature steadier
than air's, and like others, this ices over
from perimeter to center. Our edges,
fragile in the days, also froze first.
I am not one for displays, but I am
one for "To hell with it." One of me
takes a palm-sized chunk and sidearms it east,
quick-spinning fragment sliding along span.
Another me does the same, another,
another, our motions like chants: stoop, rise,
sling. The thinnest ones shatter before going
far, but they are transparent layers
on top of a vast opacity,
and there might be a lesson in that.
When I move to the big slabs, I feel them
in my gut when I throw. They stay solid
when they fall, wider revolutions,
accelerating upon impact (and we
smile at all that) out to the center which will
stay frozen longer, more deeply, floating
on itself. It'll take a little more time
than here, as we keep throwing. It just takes time.

Lake George is managed by the NYS Department of Environmental Conservation, and is a year-round destination, with boating and swimming during the summertime, colorful fall foliage, and skiing and other winter sports in the Adirondack Mountains.

Winter
Lake Erie, New York

By Mary Christine Kane

The uncles
have been out on the ice again.
They bring home trout
which grandma will bread and fry.
Their bodies turn the kitchen cold.
We breathe in chill.

Below Freezing

By Celeste Emmons

Lake Tahoe is the second deepest lake in the United States, and is located in the Sierra Nevada range in California and Nevada; historically, the area was part of a transcontinental route for railroads and later motorists, which led to its growth as a tourist destination.

Never grew
cold enough to miss you

without winter.
Just a little wind in Sacramento

every year. Our
lives were heavy then,

a quilt
I couldn't lift.

When I left, you
rented a cabin at Lake Tahoe. We

wore rain boots
in the snow until our feet turned black,

smoked cigars
to celebrate having lungs.

The temperature
dropped, but couldn't shake

us awake.
It was so late by the time

the seasons changed.
I ought to have loved you then

wooled warm
under the blanket, so

alive just the way
I would have wanted.

Sawtooth Mts

By Jack C. Buck

The day after our wedding I sold my car
to one of my best friends for 800 bucks and
said goodbye to Denver. We packed up Sam's car
with our clothes, books, pots and pans and drove
900 miles to western Idaho. After the shock, high excitement
and sleepless daze we finished unpacking and looked around
at our new place knowing we had changed our course for the better.
The following morning we elected to do something familiar
so of course we went camping. In our half torn up
1993 Road Atlas that we refuse to replace
we decided on a spot north up in McCall along Redfish Lake.
Didn't find this out until afterward but we stayed
at the same campground where Richard Brautigan wrote
two of his books while on a honeymoon in the 1960s.
The newlyweds thought the location so beautiful they stayed for a month.
We made it home for two nights. We swam, canoed, fished,
cooked over the fire, napped in the hammock, read, etc.
On the third day I tried out our new camera gifted for our wedding.
On our hike I took a photo of the Sawtooth Mountains
and later framed it in our living room. When I look at it now,
it fills me with both joy and sadness.
Not break your heart level sadness but emotionally sad.
Joy because of taking a chance, trusting a decision
and knowing there's beauty everywhere.
Sadness because the mountains remind me of Colorado
and when I mean it reminds me of Colorado
I mean it reminds me of The Rocky Mountains
because it is The Rocky Mountains. And when I see
those beautiful peaks rising to the heaven of space
it reminds me of my friends and how we made a pact
when we first all met that we didn't want to be apart for long
so in agreement we would all someday move west
together like a band to a place like Colorado, and never leave.

Looking Up

By Dorothy Swoope

Silver glint
of wings
in flight
cast confetti
across
the cerulean sky.

Part of the Rocky Mountains, these stunning peaks received their namesake from glacial action, carving and cutting with ice and rock. Also, the range is the final resting place of Ernest Hemingway, a long time visitor to the region.

Glacier National Park, Montana. Photo by Derek Wright.

Fieldnotes in February at Dawn

By Nicole Robinson

What you hoped to find,
what you longed for and couldn't
let go, a pink and purple
sunrise over a frozen lake
where deer stand below
the scotch pines
highlighted by snow,
won't be here,
won't wake you
into wonder. Instead,
a cloud cover
low enough it greys
the tops of trees as dawn ends
and light begins to slide
onto the frozen landscape,
the way you opened yourself
to yourself until
you realized you arrived
where you didn't know
you needed to be
but knew it was right

because you could breathe.
Strange how change happens
so slowly you forget
you're noticing
the colors of green
against the white of snow.
Look at how light crawls in.
What are you doing—
Where is the heart when—
The questions stutter
their fragments
and you're the loud one here.
What if the lack of footprints
could be enough?
What if you could become
what you see: stillness
in the spruces
even with the weight
of snow. Let go
of your longing
and listen:
silence until
the first chirps
of a dark-eyed junco.
Sign of waking life,
sign of singing
what you didn't know
you knew.

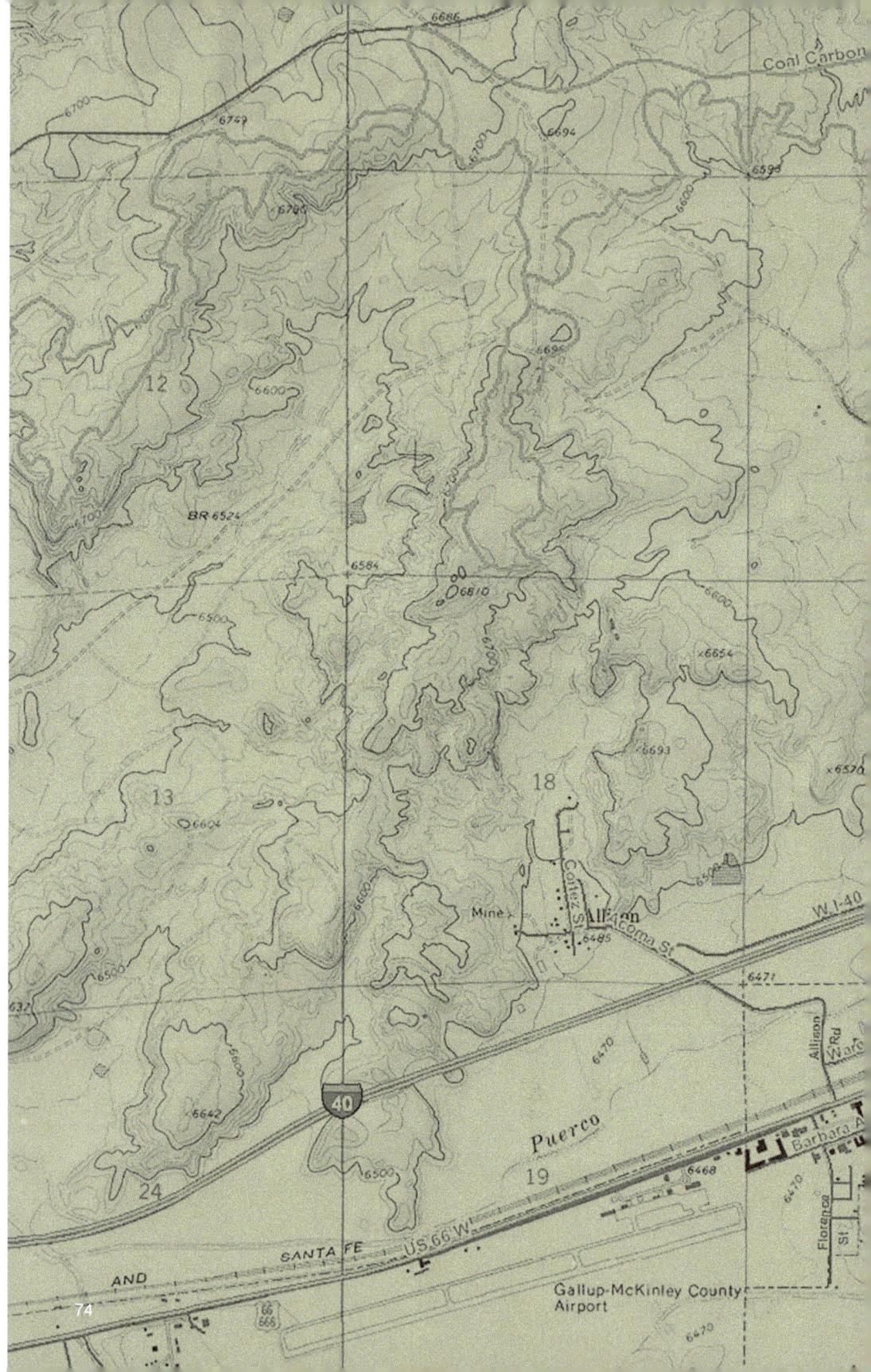

IV.
Deserts and Canyons

Part IV. Heat and Rock: Deserts and Canyons

The desert has the same immensity and biodiversity as other wild regions—the vastness of the ocean, the knitted web of water and life within the forest, and the expanse and protection of rugged, mountainous, wilderness. The desert embodies a different kind of extremity though. The sparseness of water and extremes in temperature mean that only some species of flora and fauna will thrive—some soils and plants take decades to grow, unlike the quick growth and regeneration that happens within a forest. Time slows down, but does not stop. The desert moves with sand and wind, in a system of constant, methodical, and gradual change.

The U.S. finds itself with four unique deserts in the West, Great Basin, Chihuahuan, Mojave, and Sonoran, and parts of the Columbia Basin are categorized as a "cold desert." These places offer an assemblage of parks with stark, vast, and dramatic geology, and flora and fauna necessitating critical protection—among them, Death Valley and Joshua Tree in California, White Sands National Park in New Mexico, Great Basin in Nevada and Great Sand Dunes in Colorado, Petrified Forest and Saguaro National Parks in Arizona, as well as others.

Petrified Forest National Park, Arizona. Photo by Derek Wright.

Grand Canyon National Park, Arizona. Photo by Sharon Mollerus. (CC BY 2.0)

The Grand Canyon

Considered one of the seven natural wonders of the world, Grand Canyon National Park is simply breathtaking. While many of us (especially city dwellers) spend time looking up at things, like trees, buildings, and clouds, it's rare to be able to look so far down into the earth. The joy of the park is also being able to look backward in time through the millennia as the rock layers tell the story of earth from almost two billion years ago. The river, in this context, is the newcomer, only a few million years old.

Me in My Jet Fighter

By Robert McHugh

Above Grand Canyon
Some thirty-five thousand feet
Earth's fractured landscape

Number 395
(Ghost Ranch, Abiquiu, New Mexico)

By Debbie Theiss

"Sometimes you can only say with color what you cannot express in words."
—Georgia O'Keefe

My camera's shutter clicks a fourth, then fifth photo,
the lens attempts to capture Ghost
Ranch; its burnt shades on folding mountains,
red-brick mudstone, tan sandstone.

But snapshots blur the lone cottonwood,
bent as if quenching its thirst in a spring, wearing a crown
of harvest moon. Autumn foliage hides its branches.
Golden-red and tangerine-yellow leaves blush in the setting sun.

I pick up my journal, write pasty phrases unequal
to saturated hues of the tree. Then, I remember O'Keefe—
her color chart—over 500 colors, always with her as she paints.

I note 395, 397, 398.

Last Gaze on Desert Outlook, Grand Canyon

By Phillip Bannowsky

Two desert ravens over Grand Canyon mating.
Black feathers, clear mid-morning blue,
an immense illusion
in colored bands drops below. They race
above the tourists near the rim
and fly out. Buff plateaux miles beyond
are the tint of Joanie's skin. She takes pictures
as I gaze down the shrinking juniper and pinion pine:
a green rash upon the distant outcroppings. I gasp
at the height, the space, the falling
of ravens into it. Attacked,
one folds and tumbles sideways
towards the hidden
Colorado.
Endless seconds. The shiny wings unwrap,
catch the dry air and up, up, counterattack.
Farther and farther out they
spiral and dash
until lost in the whorls of heat or perhaps
my sun-dazzled eyes. I squint north.

The river
leaks from a hazy V and disappears.

Wiping the moisture from my lashes,
I turn to Joanie, a back-lit shadow in the glare,
and take her hand to leave, heading east.
At sunset the Painted Desert, tomorrow
the Pueblo ruins, and then the Plains . . .

When I sit again beneath the shade
of beech and poplar on White Clay Creek,
"How will I remember this?"

Metamorphism

By Katherine L. Hester

Know The Canyon's History, Study Rocks Made By Time
Is what the sunburnt river runner said
At the Three Mile Resthouse

As we were coming out.
Because the shift and settle, wrench
And uplift

Are a largess
We can neither grip or grasp
Without resorting to mnemonics.

Dust and heat and sky and shadow;
Shale, limestone and sandstone–
From small to large and back again,

All has been ground down
Into the finest powder
Of its elements.

We went down by one trail.
Came up by another.
The canyon wrung us out,

Exerted pressure, burned off
The unnecessary,
Left the best,

The whippoorwill's call,
The scouring red dust.
The implacable mineral gleam
Of water birthed,
From the very bottom of the dam.

Red Rock Canyon National Conservation Area, Nevada. Photo by Amy Beth Wright.

The Columbia River Basin is 150 miles inland from the Pacific Northwest coast and stretches more than 200 miles eastward, between massive continental forests, with few trees. It is flat, arid, and referred to as a "cool desert."

Balsamroot in the Columbia Basin

By Francis Opila

The night of the hard frost, the icy moon showers its cold light on the rock soil, the dawn brings red-winged blackbirds singing among meadowlarks. You wonder, what song do you sing on the edge of your love, as you thaw, opening to balsamroot in bloom, their sunny faces splash gold over the sagebrush steppe, along the basalt cliffs, desert parsley, prairie lupine, you know your way home, but you're still adrift, deep shadows sink on the Columbia below, wind on the edge of the precipice, turkey vultures soar on thermals and gusts.

Joshua Tree National Park, California.
Photo by Derek Wright.

A Stillness Rose

By Carol Deering

First hike down   a stumble,
new boots in bluish light.
I stand up dizzy, staring

past rippled stone to water,
through rippling water to stone,
the setting sun
angling prismatic.

Full-moon switchbacks,
purple shadow walls,
the light changes

and I start over
differently. I need the turns,
the time, the roar
of the blazing river

imprinted on my mind.

Being at Indian Canyon, Agua Caliente, CA

By Pamela Ahlen

Rocks rest
like tilted pillows, behemoth beds.
Birds rest, no breeze ruffling their feathers
or the pleats of skirted palms.
I rest, too, prop an injured foot,
trying to put disappointment aside,
needing a good swig of cactus juice
to let the day be what it will
beyond my hunger to devour the place,
trek off and scramble every nook, crack
and slab. Instead, I gobble up the view:
mouthfeel of almond olive honeycomb,
toasted flax, gingersnap—
for once, not trying to control how
the desert would go on without me,
why I'm splayed like a lizard
beneath the lemonade sun.

The Indian Canyons outside of Palm Springs are sacred tribal lands of the Agua Caliente Band of Cahuilla Indians. The area is home to a seasonal 60-foot waterfall, 150 species of plant life, ancient irrigation systems and trading posts, endangered species such as the Least Bells Vireo bird and the Peninsular Bighorn Sheep, and footpaths to gorges and other geologic formations.

Big Bend National Park, Texas. Photo by Liz Paul.

Big Bend and the Rio Grande

One of the largest of the national parks in the lower 48, Big Bend, is also one of the most remote, a five-hour drive from the nearest larger city, El Paso. This park celebrates and protects the unique ecosystem of the Rio Grande River, while also preserving ancient settlements and a wealth of canyons and geologic features, including 500-million year old rocks, remnants of three mountain-building episodes in North America, and the longest fossil record of any national park unit. The park is one of the few situated on an international border; the river provides not only the southern boundary for the park but also the Mexico-U.S. border.

Photograph of You Straddling Two Countries

By Allyson Whipple

The Rio Grande is only shin-deep, but the current
almost pulls me to my knees as I try to take
your picture. We're both wincing, pebbles stabbing
the soles of our feet in the rushing water. You stand
in your Walt Whitman hat, grin, ask *Which side am I on?*
Beyond the frame, you'll step
onto the Mexican riverbank, no fear
of the border patrol helicopters that tore
across the sky ten minutes earlier. You stare
at the sheer cliff of the Santa Elena canyon,
rising from rocks behind your back, say,
Any politician who thinks he can build a wall
has never seen the border.

Yesterday, on the Boquillas Canyon trail,
we saw carved walking sticks, painted rocks, a handwritten price
list in Spanish, a collection bowl. Items for sale, but nobody to watch
for theft, nobody to make change. An invisible artist slipping
across boundaries, undeterred, the blades of the Airbus A-Star
chopping through the desert. I wish I'd bought
something, wish I'd let her know which side I was on.

For the Escape and the Bonding

By Elizabeth Paul

We went to nature again, to Big Bend,
for the heat and the strangeness
of cacti, mountains,
and javelina.

The worst part was when we summited Emory Peak,
the last ten minutes bouldering with a bulky
backpack messing with my balance, my
wedding ring scraping against each
hold, the top narrow and windy,
and I too dizzy to
look around.
I felt old.
When I was young and single, I thought,
I might have felt freaked out, but I
knew then how to ignore it.
But I wasn't sure
that was true.

The best part was when we swam in our underwear in the Rio Grande.
We waited for the canoe groups to go by, the river just a narrow
current there, so shallow the boats scraped against
the stones. Then we piled our clothes
like soft cairns and waded in.
You showed me how to do a push up to dunk myself in shallow water,
something you learned from your uncle who drowned in a river
almost a year ago and half way around the world,
disappeared like you once did,
500 miles up this same
Rio Grande.
We were rafting, and you fell in, completely submerged.
It was just for a moment, but in that moment,
I couldn't believe how quickly and
entirely you were gone
from my world.

On the drive home, we pulled over at the immigration check point.
And where were you born, the soldier asked you.
I forget that you have an accent.
It never occurred to me
to bring our
passports.
But I'm a born and raised American,
which was apparent to the soldier,
who trusted in fragile
belongings and
waved us
on.

Reflecting Pools

By Lois Marie Harrod

What water can do, still itself and mirror—
small pools on sandstone contemplating
rock and sky. Each its own Claude mirror

returning the reaches. What is back and beyond,
too high to touch, they contain.
Perhaps you've known it too, in a street,

water gathering to a glass that doesn't drop or shatter.
Consider the distance rain falls to be here—
you do not understand your existence either.

But here you are at this one time and place
and not some other elsewhere. How lucky
you didn't die of those childhood diseases,

strep and pertussis, how lucky your children,
grandchildren too, liquid on this earth,
the wild sky turning in their eyes.

Arches National Park, Utah. Photo by Derek Wright.

Written in Stone

By Atreyee Gupta

The durability of Estrada sandstone
seeps into me.

My arms swell into immovable vermillion arches
framing infinity.

Feet form fixed monoliths atop
evaporite basin.

Skin crinkles along anticlines,
austere, permanent.

I transpose into inert, unyielding rock.

Yet, underneath the adamantine composition time corrodes:
arid heat cracks through sedimentary layers;
wind abrades lithic fragments;
rain seeps into fissures,
freezes,
gnaws through feldspar grains.

I too am transforming:
sloughing off epithelium and vanity,
shedding muscle and hubris,
eroding bone
and ego.

My disintegration written in stone.

Arches National Park, Utah. Photo by Amy Beth Wright.

Epilogue

Charles M. Russell National Wildlife Refuge, Montana. Photo by Derek Wright.

Asset Protection

By Susan Marsh

Let us secure our assets:
Bright, laundry-day air
Water we can drink
A place to walk and daydream
The rush of water, the quiet pulse
Of the earth and those who share it:
Ants and otters, earwigs and eagles,
Birch and aspen, lichen and seaweed,
Ourselves and one another.

Let us manage our wealth:
Land that can keep giving
To all who come to receive,
Creeks that meander and deepen
Sedge at their margins knitting
Them into place, trout
Dreaming in their shadows,
Forests that mature and decay
And spill their dividends to the future.
They will only grow in value.

The Trail Back

By Gene Twaronite

is never the same.
The sun you once faced
is now over your shoulder,
the horizon where you're
headed is now the one
where you've been.
You follow your footprints
as you explore the world
made new in hindsight
hoping to find what it is
you have missed.

The Poets

Pamela Ahlen is program coordinator for Bookstock Literary Festival held each summer in Woodstock, Vermont. She organizes literary events for Osher (Lifelong Education at Dartmouth) and compiled and edited Osher's Anthology of *Poets and Writers: Celebrating Twenty-Five Years at Dartmouth*. Pam received an MFA from Vermont College of Fine Arts and is the author of the chapbook *Gather Every Little Thing* (Finishing Line Press).

Mary Ardery is originally from Bloomington, IN. Her work appears or is forthcoming in *Missouri Review's* "Poem of the Week," *Fairy Tale Review*, *Cincinnati Review's* "miCRo" series, *Prairie Schooner, Salt Hill*, and elsewhere. She holds an MFA from Southern Illinois University-Carbondale, where she won an Academy of American Poets Prize. You can visit her at maryardery.com.

Phillip Bannowsky is a retired autoworker, international educator, and 2017 Delaware Division of the Arts Established Artist Fellow in poetry. His published works include *The Milk of Human Kindness (poetry), Autoplant: a Poetic Monologue, The Mother Earth Inn* (novel), and *Jacobo the Turko: a Novel in Verses*. He has recently retired as an adjunct at the University of Delaware, where he last taught "The Poetry of Empowerment." This poem appeared in issue nine of *Dreamstreets,* August 1989.

Karen Berry lives and works in Portland, Oregon. Her work has appeared in *Goblin Fruit, Panorama Journal, Ekphrastic Review, Subprimal, Indiana Voice, Prairie Poetry, Napalm and Novocaine,* and many more print and online journals. She is a poet and a novelist, but pays the mortgage as a marketing writer. More information about her work is available at https://karengberry.mywriting.network.

Gary Bloom has published articles, poetry, photography, and fiction in numerous print and online magazines, including *Breath and Shadow, American Visions, Milwaukee Magazine, The Buffalo News, The Grand Rapids Press, Grit, Cappers, Oasis, Mankato Poetry Review, Players,* and *Black Diaspora.* He grew up in Minneapolis and has Bachelor's and

Master's degrees from Mankato (Minnesota) State University. After working for many years as a computer programmer and database administrator he now lives and writes in Pass Christian, Mississippi. This poem appeared in *Oasis* in 1993.

Jack C. Buck currently lives in Boise, Idaho. He is the author of the collections *Deer Michigan, Gathering View,* and *will you let it send you out*.

Jeff Burt lives in Santa Cruz County, California with his wife. He works in mental health. He has contributed to *Rabid Oak, Tar River Poetry Review, Williwaw Journal, Cold Mountain Review,* and *Sheila-na-Gig*.

Pamela Hobart Carter loves how close the Cascades are to Seattle. Summers she hikes in them, winters she skis in them. She has always been interested in rocks and has two geology degrees, from Indiana University and Bryn Mawr College. Her poetry chapbooks: *Her Imaginary Museum* and *Held Together with Tape and Glue*. Find more about Carter at www.playwrightpam.wordpress.com.

Amanda Lin Costa is a New York-based writer, artist and filmmaker. Her wanders in national parks often inspire her work. She's been known to write poems in the middle of the night and furiously between subway stops. You can follow her work at theloneolive.com.

Carol L. Deering has twice received the Wyoming Arts Council Poetry Fellowship (2016, judge Rebecca Foust; 1999, judge Agha Shahid Ali). Her poems appear in online and traditional journals and anthologies, and in her first book, published fall 2018: *Havoc & Solace: Poems from the Inland West* (Sastrugi Press) https://www.sastrugipress.com/books/havoc-and-solace/.

Ann DeVilbiss has work published or forthcoming in *Columbia Journal, Crab Orchard Review, Gertrude, The Maine Review, Painted Bride Quarterly, PANK,* and elsewhere. Her chapbook, *When the Wolves Stay Quiet,* is available from dancing girl press, and she lives and works in Louisville, Kentucky.

Iris Jamahl Dunkle is an award-winning poet, literary biographer, and essayist. She has published four poetry books, including *West: Fire: Archive* (The Center for Literary Publishing, 2021) and the biography *Charmian Kittredge London: Trailblazer, Author, Adventurer*. Dunkle teaches at Napa Valley College and is the Poetry Director at the Napa Valley Writers' Conference.

Susan Melinda Dunlap is a fiction writer, playwright and poet. *Bright Bones: An Anthology of Contemporary Montana Writers,* included her short story, "The Haunting of Butte." *The Piltsdown Review* featured her as a poet and *The Alexandria Quarterly* published one of her poems in an anthology, *End of Summer Poems.* She has also been published by Word Riot. The Root and the Bloom and Eye/Land Institute have commissioned her to write plays. Orphan Girl Children's Theatre performed her play *The Good Slipper* through Zoom. A maximum-security prison outside of Los Angeles performed her play *The Dog Ghost,* as did Montana Repertory Theater. Her work has also been seen at the Last Chance Gulch New Play Fest, the William Inge Festival, the Fringe Festival, 13th Street Theater, Dixon Place and performed by Project in Motion. MFA: Brooklyn College, where she received the Louis B. Goodman Creative Writing Scholarship.

Sara Eddy has published two chapbooks of poetry—*Tell the Bees* (A3 Press, 2019) and *Full Mouth* (Finishing LIne Press, 2020). Her poems have appeared in the *Baltimore Review, Spank the Carp,* and *Threepenny Review,* among numerous other publications. She is Assistant Director of the Jacobson Center for Writing at Smith College, and lives in Amherst, Massachusetts with two teenagers, a black cat, a white dog, and three beehives. She is currently at work on the next thing, but she's not sure what exactly it is, yet.

Celeste Emmons Celeste Emmons (MFA, Sarah Lawrence '16) is a creative living in the Hudson Valley with her husband, three cats, and daughter Ivy. By day, she is an academic advisor and sometimes-professor at SUNY Ulster. The rest of the time, she is making things and exploring various wildernesses.

Andy Fogle is the author of *Across from Now,* six chapbooks of poetry, with other poems, co-translations, collage, and a variety of nonfiction in *Anomaly, Blackbird, Chicago Quarterly Review, Gargoyle, Image, Parks and*

Points, Right Hand Pointing, and elsewhere, with music on Bandcamp. He's from Virginia, and now lives in upstate NY.

Laura Foley is the author of six poetry collections, including, most recently, *WTF* and *Night Ringing.* Her poem "Gratitude List" won the Common Good Books poetry contest and was read by Garrison Keillor on *The Writer's Almanac*. Her poem "Nine Ways of Looking at Light" won the Joe Gouveia Outermost Poetry Contest, judged by Marge Piercy. Her book, *The Glass Tree,* won a Foreword Review Prize for Poetry. Her poems have also appeared in Valparaiso Poetry Review, DMQ, Room Magazine, McClellan Poetry Prize Website, Pittsburgh Poetry Review, Bellevue Literary Review, in the anthologies, *Aesthetica Creative Writing, In the Arms of Words: Poems for Disaster Relief, Ice Cream Poems, Roads Taken: Contemporary Vermont Poets, Not My President, an anthology of Dissent,* and others. A palliative-care volunteer in hospitals, with an M.A. and a M. Phil. in English Lit. from Columbia University, she lives with her wife and their two dogs among the hills of Vermont.

Christine Gelineau is the author of three books of poetry: *Crave* (NYQ Books); *Appetite for the Divine and Remorseless Loyalty* (both from Ashland Poetry Press). A recipient of the Pushcart Prize, Gelineau teaches in the low-residency MFA at Wilkes University; after 26 years there, she has just retired from Binghamton University. Her poetry, essays, and reviews have appeared widely including in *Prairie Schooner, New Letters, The New York Times* Opinionator, *Green Mountains Review* and others.

Mike Good lives in Pittsburgh and serves as managing editor at Autumn House Press. Some of his recent poetry and book reviews can be found in or are forthcoming at *december, Five Points, Full Stop, Ploughshares, Salamander, SOFTBLOW, Waxwing,* and elsewhere. His work has received support from the Sewanee Writers' Conference and *The Sun,* and he holds an MFA from Hollins University.

Atreyee Gupta is a writer exploring the liminal spaces in which humans interact with society, geography, and nature. Atreyee is the creator of Bespoke Traveler, a digital alcove examining travel's transformative power. Atreyee's work has been published in *Arc Poetry, Blue Cubicle Press, Jaggery, Shanghai Literary Review,* and *The Sunlight Press,* among others.

U.S. poet Lois Marie Harrod's 17th collection *Woman* was published by Blue Lyra in February 2020. *Nightmares of the Minor Poet* appeared in June 2016 from Five Oaks; her chapbook *And She Took the Heart* appeared in January 2016; *Fragments from the Biography of Nemesis* (Cherry Grove Press) and the chapbook *How Marlene Mae Longs for Truth* (Dancing Girl Press) appeared in 2013. A Dodge poet, she is published in literary journals and online ezines from *American Poetry Review* to *Zone 3*. She teaches online at the Evergreen Forum in Princeton; before the pandemic she taught at The College of New Jersey. Links to online work www.loismarieharrod.org

Katherine L. Hester only recently started submitting poetry; she has had poems published in *Southwest Review, Ruminate, Places @ DesignObserver* and *Flyway*. *Eggs for Young America,* her first collection of short stories, was awarded a Katharine Nason Bakeless Literary Publication Prize for Fiction and chosen as a *New York Times* Notable Book. Her fiction has been published in quarterlies including *American Short Fiction, Five Points, The Yale Review, Shenandoah, Crazyhorse* and anthologized in *Prize Stories: The O. Henry Awards* and *Best American Mystery Stories*.

Emily Alta Hockaday is a Queens-based poet and editor. Her newest chapbook, *Beach Vocabulary*, is forthcoming from Red Bird Chaps. She is author of *Space on Earth* (Grey Book Press), *Ophelia: A Botanist's Guide* (Zoo Cake Press), *What We Love & Will Not Give Up* (Dancing Girl Press), and *Starting a Life* (Finishing Line Press). She can be found on the web at www.emilyhockaday.com and @E_Hockaday.

Alicia Hokanson's first collection of poems, *Mapping the Distance,* was selected by Carolyn Kizer for a King County Arts Commission publication prize. Two chapbooks from Brooding Heron Press are *Insistent in the Skin* and *Phosphorous*. Her newest collection, *Perishable World,* will be out from Pleasure Boat Studio in the spring of 2021. She was named the River of Words Poetry Teacher of the Year in 2003. Now retired after a long career teaching English, she devotes her time to writing, tutoring, and political activism in Seattle and on Waldron Island, Washington.

Mary Christine Kane grew up in Western New York and has lived in Twin Cities most of her adult life. She works in marketing and is a volunteer for the arts and animal rescue. She earned her MFA from Hamline University. *Between the stars where you are lost,* her poetry chapbook, was published by Finishing Line Press in 2019. Her poetry and nonfiction has also appeared in journals and anthologies including *Bluestem; The Buffalo Anthology, Right Here, Right Now; Sleet, Ponder Review* and others.

Susan Marsh lives in Jackson, Wyoming. Marsh's writing explores our human ability to discover the secrets within the land and ourselves through encounters with wild nature, and how we change as a result. Marsh worked for over 30 years as a public land steward in the Bridger-Teton National Forest. Her poems have appeared in *Clerestory, Dark Matter, Manzanita Review,* and other journals.

Robert McHugh is a native of Baltimore, Maryland and a former U.S.A.F. navigator during WWII, and a jet fighter pilot during the Korean War. He is a retired sales and marketing consultant with a B.A. from Princeton and an M.B.A. from NYU. He has been a GrandPals senior reading to Kindergarteners at five different elementary schools in Hopewell-Lawrenceville-Princeton, New Jersey area for the last five years, and is a poet and memoirist.

Kathleen Meadows was born in Bakersfield, California, and grew up in the rural San Joaquin Valley. She holds degrees from U.C. Santa Barbara and U.C. Berkeley in English and has taught in schools throughout the Bay Area. Since retiring, Kathleen has studied poetry at the Writing Salon in San Francisco with Kathleen McClung and at Berkeley City College, and in 2019, she received honorable mention commendations in two categories for the Soul-Making Keats literary competition. She lives in the El Cerrito hills, her backyard a grove of redwood trees overlooking the San Francisco Bay and Mt. Tamalpais.

Kevin Oberlin teaches at the University of Cincinnati, Blue Ash College, and is the author of the chapbook *Spotlit Girl* (2008).

Rebecca Hart Olander's poetry has appeared recently in *Crab Creek Review, Ilanot Review, Mom Egg Review, Plath Poetry Project, Radar Poetry, Solstice, Yemassee Journal,* and others. Her chapbook, *Dressing the Wounds,* was published by dancing girl press in 2019, and her first full-length collection, *Uncertain Acrobats,* is out with CavanKerry Press in 2021. Rebecca lives in Western Massachusetts where she teaches writing at Westfield State University and is editor and director of Perugia Press. You can find her at rebeccahartolander.com and @rholanderpoet.

Francis Opila has lived in the Pacific Northwest most of his adult life; he currently resides in Portland, OR. His work, recreation, and spirit have taken him out into the woods, wetlands, rivers, mountains, and deserts. He works in environmental science, primarily with water quality. His poems have appeared in *Windfall, Clackamas Literary Review, Willawaw Journal, Soul-Lit,* in addition to other journals. He enjoys performing poetry, combining recitation and playing Native American flute.

Carl "Papa" Palmer of Old Mill Road in Ridgeway, Virginia, lives in University Place, Washington. He is retired from the military and Federal Aviation Administration (FAA) enjoying life as "Papa" to his grand descendants and being a Franciscan Hospice volunteer. Carl is a Pushcart Prize, Best of the Net and Micro Award nominee. Papa's MOTTO: Long Weekends Forever!

Elizabeth Paul has an MFA in creative writing from Vermont College of Fine Arts, and her texts and images have appeared in *Cold Mountain Review, Carolina Quarterly, Sweet Lit, The Indianapolis Review,* and elsewhere. Her chapbook *Reading Girl* is a collection of ekphrastic prose poems based on paintings by Henri Matisse. Liz served as a Peace Corps volunteer in Kyrgyzstan and currently teaches writing at George Mason University. Learn more at elizabethsgpaul.com.

Kristin Bryant Rajan, PhD in English, writes poetry, fiction, creative nonfiction, and literary criticism in Atlanta, GA. She is widely published in creative writing journals and anthologies as well as academic journals. She is a Pushcart and Best of the Net nominee. Her criticism investigates Buddhism and meditative moments of deep self in modernist literature. She teaches English at Kennesaw State University, facilitates happiness workshops for faculty, students, and community groups, and also teaches spin classes at the YMCA. Her daily meditation practice inspires her writing, research, teaching, and life.

Cinthia Ritchie is an Alaska writer, ultra-runner and three-time Pushcart Prize nominee who spends a ridiculous amount of time running mountains with a dog named Seriously. Find her work at *New York Times Magazine, Evening Street Review, Sport Literate, Rattle, Best American Sports Writing, Mary, Into the Void, Clementine Unbound, Deaf Poets Society, Forgotten Women* anthology, *Nasty Women* anthology, *Gyroscope Review, Bosque Literary Journal, The Hunger Journal* and others. Her first novel *Dolls Behaving Badly* was published by Hachette Book Group and her memoir will be published this fall by Raised Voice Press. www.cinthiaritchie.com

Nicole Robinson's poetry has appeared in *Great River Review, Columbia Journal, Tahoma Literary Review, The Fourth River,* and elsewhere. She has received an Individual Excellence Award for poetry from the Ohio Arts Council and serves on the board for Lit Youngstown. Robinson holds an MFA in poetry from Ashland University and is currently the narrative medicine coordinator at Akron Children's Hospital.

Marian Kaplun Shapiro grew up in a housing project in The Bronx. She rejoices in her life as a psychologist in Lexington, Massachusetts where her house and office look out on the grass, the trees, the birds, and the clear sky. And in summer she returns with her husband, adult children and their children to Rangeley, Maine, where she writes, reads, walks, and canoes for three glorious weeks. She is the author of a professional book, *Second Childhood* (Norton, 1988); two chapbooks: *Your Third Wish,* (Finishing Line, 2007); and *The End Of The World, Announced On Wednesday* (Pudding House, 2007); and two poetry collections, *Players In The Dream, Dreamers In The Play* (Plain View Press, 2007) and her new book of experimental poetry, *At The Edge Of The Cliff* (also Plain View Press, 2021) Marian is a five-time Senior Poet Laureate of Massachusetts. She was nominated for the Pushcart Prize in 2012.

Sarah Stern is the author of *We Have Been Lucky in the Midst of Misfortune* (Kelsay Press, Aldrich Press, 2018), *But Today Is Different* (Wipf and Stock Publishers, 2014) and *Another Word For Love* (Finishing Line Press, 2011). She is a recipient of two Pushcart Prize nominations and a five-time winner of the Bronx Council on the Arts BRIO Poetry Award. You can see more of her work at https://sarahstern.me/.

Virginia Chase Sutton's second book, *What Brings You to Del Amo,* winner of the Morse Poetry Prize, was recently reissued as a free ebook by Doubleback Books/Sundress. *Embellishments* was her first book, *Of a Transient Nature* was her third, and *Down River* was her chapbook. Sutton's poems have won a scholarship to Bread Loaf, the Allen Ginsberg Poetry Award, and the National Poet Hunt, among many other prizes, awards, and residencies. Eight times nominated for a Pushcart Prize, her poems have appeared in *The Paris Review, Ploughshares, Mom Egg Review, Cortland Review, Glass Literary Journal,* and many other literary magazines, journals, and anthologies. She has an MA in literature and an MFA from Vermont College of Fine Arts in Poetry. She lives in Tempe, Arizona, where she teaches adult students in writing and spends her time writing poetry and some prose.

Dorothy Swoope is an award winning poet whose works have been published in print and online in newspapers, anthologies and literary magazines in Australian, the U.S.A. and Canada. Her memoir, *Wait 'til Your Father Gets Home!* was published in 2016. She resides on the South Coast of New South Wales, Australia.

Debbie Theiss lives in Lee's Summit, Missouri, grew up in the Midwest, and finds inspiration for her poetry in the unfolding art of daily life and nature. She has poems published in *I-70 Review, Skinny Journal, Kansas Time and Place, Interpretations IV & V, Helen Literary Journal, River & South Review, Postcard Poems and Prose, Star 82 Review, Weaving the Terrain* from Dos Gatos Press, and others.

Marjorie Thomsen loves teaching others how to play with words and live more poetically in the world. She is the author of *Pretty Things Please* (Turning Point, 2016). Two poems from this collection were read on *The Writer's Almanac*. One of Marjorie's poems about hiking in a dress and high heels was made into a short animated film. She has been nominated three times for a Pushcart Prize and Best of the Net. She is the recipient of poetry awards from the University of Iowa School of Social Work, *Poetica Magazine*, and others. Publications include *Pangyrus, Rattle, SWWIM*, and *Tupelo Quarterly*. Marjorie has been a Poet in Residence in schools throughout New England. She is a psychotherapist and instructor at Boston University's School of Social Work.

Kerry Trautman's poetry and fiction have appeared in various journals, including *The Fourth River, Alimentum, Midwestern Gothic,* and *Think*

Journal, as well as in anthologies such as *Mourning Sickness* (Omniarts, 2008,) and *Journey to Crone* (Chuffed Buff Books, 2013.) Her chapbooks are *Things That Come in Boxes* (Kingcraft Press 2012,) *To Have Hoped* (Finishing Line Press 2015,) *Artifacts* (Night Ballet Press 2017,) and *To Be Nonchalantly Alive* (Kelsay Books 2020.)

Gene Twaronite is a Tucson poet, essayist, and children's fiction writer. He is the author of ten books, including two juvenile fantasy novels as well as collections of essays, short stories, and poems, and the picture book *How to Eat Breakfast*. His first poetry book *Trash Picker on Mars* was the winner of the 2017 New Mexico-Arizona Book Award for Arizona poetry. Other poetry collections include *The Museum of Unwearable Shoes* and *What the Gargoyle Sees,* published by Kelsay Books. Follow more of Gene's writing at his website: thetwaronitezone.com.

Kory Wells is the author of *Sugar Fix,* poetry from Terrapin Books. Her writing has been featured on *The Slowdown* poetry podcast and appears in *Ruminate, Stirring, The Southern Poetry Anthology,* and elsewhere. A recent poet laureate of Murfreesboro, Tennessee, Kory nurtures connection and community through her writing and advocacy for the arts, democracy, afternoon naps, and other good causes. korywells.com

Pat Phillips West's poems have been published in various journals including *Haunted Waters Press, Clover, A Literary Rag, San Pedro River Review, Slipstream, Gold Man Review,* and elsewhere. She is a multiple Pushcart nominee and a Best of the Net nominee.

Allyson Whipple is the author of *Come into the World Like That* (Five Oaks Press, 2016) and *We're Smaller Than We Think We Are* (Finishing Line Press, 2013) and co-author of the interactive fiction *Choice: Texas* (www.playchoicetexas.com, 2014). Her poetry is informed by the landscape and political climate of Texas. She serves on the board of *Borderlands: Texas Poetry Review*. Allyson teaches technical communication at Austin Community College.

Martin Willitts Jr is a retired librarian who has been a primitive camper and has visited almost all the national parks. He has 21 full-length collections including the Blue Light Press Award winner in 2019, *The Temporary World*. His forthcoming book is *Harvest Time* (Deerbrook

Press, 2021).

Sally Zakariya's poetry has appeared in some 75 print and online journals and has been nominated for the Pushcart Prize and Best of the Net. Her most recent publication is *Muslim Wife* (Blue Lyra Press, 2019). She is also the author of *The Unknowable Mystery of Other People*, *Personal Astronomy*, *When You Escape*, *Insectomania*, and *Arithmetic* and other verses, as well as the editor of a poetry anthology, *Joys of the Table*. A former magazine writer and editor, Zakariya lives in Arlington, Virginia, with her husband and cat. She blogs at www.butdoesitrhyme.com.

Thomas Zimmerman teaches English, directs the Writing Center, and edits *The Big Windows Review* at Washtenaw Community College, in Ann Arbor, Michigan. His latest poetry chapbook is *Conjugal Spaces: A Poem*. Visit Tom's website, https://thomaszimmerman.wordpress.com.

Acknowledgements

Our utmost gratitude to the contributing poets for sharing their work in this anthology, and supporting this project from the very beginning. We are grateful as well to the many poets who have shared their work with us since we launched our poetry series in 2017. Thank you to Nicholas Wright for working with us so generously to finalize, develop, and polish our design for *Wayfinding*. With gratitude to Celeste Emmons, Parks and Points' poetry editor for the 2017 and 2018 series; her insight helped us create an annual series and shape its direction forward. Thanks to Finishing Line Press for making this book a reality, and thanks to our families and friends for supporting Parks & Points and its mission to celebrate public lands through writing. Special thanks to Melissa Faliveno, Rebecca Hart Olander, Liz Paul, and Leigh Stein for counsel that helped us to determine the course of this book. And, thanks to the incredible stewards and rangers of public lands who inspire us to learn and form connections, and to the many non-profits whose tireless advocacy protects and upholds public lands as a vital place within our culture and world.

Morris County Parks, New Jersey. Photo by Derek Wright.

About the Editors

Amy Beth Wright and **Derek Wright** created the website Parks & Points in 2016, the same year as the National Park Service celebrated its centennial. Parks & Points hosts an annual creative nonfiction contest and a spring poetry series, publishing self-reflective writing that evokes the landscapes, histories, and cultural legacies found within National Park Service units and many other diverse public lands.
Visit parksandpoints.com to read more.

Amy Beth Wright is a journalist, essayist, and writing professor. She completed her MFA in Writing at Sarah Lawrence College and teaches writing at Purchase College (SUNY Purchase). She and Derek collaborate on features about public lands for a variety of outlets.
Visit amybethwrites.com to read more of her work.

Derek Wright is a NYC-based writer, designer, and photographer. With Amy Beth, he has written for a variety of publications including *Fodors, American Wild*, and *Southwest: The Magazine*. Derek originated Parks & Points as a way to celebrate national park sites and public lands. He also works as a theatrical lighting designer and a photographer, and teaches at New York University.

www.ingramcontent.com/pod-product-compliance
Lightning Source LLC
Chambersburg PA
CBHW042144160426
43201CB00022B/2402